Forgiv
and the Cross of Christ

SOUND BOOKS PUBLISHING

FORGIVENESS
and
THE CROSS OF CHRIST

J.C. RYLE

(revised)

Worldwide Ministries 1998

Produced by Sound Books Publishing
Cheshire, England.

ISBN 1 901044 03 3

Printed by Caledonian International Book Manufacturing Co. Ltd.
Glasgow, Great Britain.

FORGIVENESS

"Your sins are forgiven you." John 2 v 12.

There is a clause near the end of the Apostle's creed, which, I fear, is often repeated without thought or consideration. I refer to the clause which contains these words, *"I believe in the forgiveness of sins."* Thousands I am afraid, never reflect what those words mean. I propose to examine the subject of them in the following paper, and I invite the attention of all who care for their souls, and want to be saved.

Do we believe in the "Resurrection of our bodies"? Then let us see to it that we know something by experience of the forgiveness of our sins.

1. Let me show, first of all, our need of forgiveness.

All men need forgiveness, because all men are sinners. He that does not know this, knows nothing in religion. It is the very A B C of Christianity, that a man should know his right place in the sight of God, and understand his 'just deserts'.

We are all great sinners. "There is none righteous, no, not one." - "All have sinned, and come short of the glory of God." (Rom. 3 v 10, 23.) Sinners we were born, and sinners we have been all our lives. We take to sin naturally from the very first.

No child ever needs schooling and education to teach it to do wrong. No devil, or bad companion, ever leads us into such wickedness as our own hearts. And "the wages of sin is death." (Rom. 6 v 23.) We must either be forgiven, or lost eternally.

We are all guilty sinners in the sight of God. We have broken His holy law. We have transgressed His precepts. We have not done His will. There is not a commandment in all the ten which does not condemn us.

If we have not broken it in word, we have in thought and imagination, - and that continually. Tried by the standard of the fifth chapter of St. Matthew, there is not one of us that would be acquitted. All the world is "guilty before God." And "as it is appointed unto men once to die, so after this comes the judgment." We must either be forgiven, or perish everlastingly. (Rom. 3 v 19; Heb. 9 v 27.)

When I walk through the crowded streets of London, I see hundreds and thousands of whom I know nothing beyond their outward appearance. I see some bent on pleasure, and some on business, - some who look rich, and some who look poor, - some rolling

along in their vehicles, some hurrying along on foot.
Each has his own object in view. Each has his own aims and ends, all alike hidden from me.

But one thing I know for a certainty, as I look upon them, - they are all sinners. There is not a holy soul among them, - they are all sinners. There is not a soul among them all but "deserves God's wrath and condemnation."
Every man or woman in that crowd must die either forgiven, or else rise again to be condemned for ever at the last day.

When I look through the length and breadth of Great Britain I must make the same report. From the Land's End to the North Foreland, - from the Isle of Wight to Caithness, - from the Queen on the throne to the worker in the factory, - we are all sinners.

At one time we Englishmen had a name among the empires of the earth. We sent our ships into every sea, and our merchandise into every town in the world. We have bridged the Atlantic with our vessels. We have made night in our cities like day with artificial light. We have changed England into one great county by railways and roads. We can exchange thought between London and Edinburgh in a few seconds by the electronic technology. But with all our arts and sciences, - with all our machinery and inventions, - with all our armies and navies, - with all our lawyers and statesmen, we have not altered the nature of our people. We are still in the eye of God an island full of sinners.

When I turn to the map of the world I must say the same thing. It matters not what quarter I examine: I find men's hearts are everywhere the same, and everywhere wicked.

Sin is the family disease of all the children of Adam. Never has there been a corner of the earth discovered where sin and the devil do not reign. Wide as the difference is between the nations of the earth, they have always been found to have one great mark in common. Europe and Asia, Africa and America, Iceland and India. Paris and Peking, - all alike have the mark of sin.

The eye of the Lord looks down on this globe of ours, as it rolls round the sun, and sees it covered with corruption and wickedness. What He sees in the moon and stars, in Jupiter and Saturn, I cannot tell, - but on the earth I know He sees sin. (Psalm 14 v 2,3.)

I have no doubt such language as this sounds extravagant to some. You think I am going much too far. But mark well what I am about to say next, and then consider whether I have not used the words of soberness and truth.

What then, I ask, is the life of the best Christian amongst us all? What is it but one great career of short-comings?

What is it but a daily acting out the words of our Prayer-book, - "leaving undone things we ought to do, and doing things that we ought not to do"? Our faith, how feeble! Our love, how cold! Our works, how few! Our zeal, how small! Our patience, how short breathed! Our humility, how threadbare! Our self-denial, how dwarfish! Our knowledge, how dim! Our spirituality, how shallow! Our prayers, how formal! Our desires for more grace, how feeble!

Never did the wisest of men speak more wisely than when he said, "There is not a just man upon earth, that doeth good, and sinneth not." (Eccles, 7 v 20.) "In many things" says the apostle James "we offend all." (James 3 v 2.) And what is the best action that is ever done by the very best of

Christians? What is it after all but an imperfect work, when tried on its own merits? It is, as Luther says, not better than "a splendid sin." It is always more or less defective. It is either wrong in its motive or incomplete in its performance, - not done from perfect principles or not executed in a perfect way. The eyes of men may see no fault in it, but weighed in the balances of God it would be found wanting, and viewed in the light of heaven it would prove full of flaws.

It is like the drop of water which seems clear to the naked eye, but, placed under a microscope, is discovered to be full of impurity. David's account is literally true: "There is none that doeth good, no, not one." (Psalm 14 v 3.)

And then what is the Lord God, whose eyes are on all our ways, and before whom we have one day to give account? "Holy, holy, holy," is the remarkable expression applied to Him by those who are nearest to Him. (Isaiah 6 v 3; Rev. 4 v 8.) It sounds as if not one word could express the intensity of His holiness. One of His prophets says, "He is of purer eyes then to behold evil, and cannot look on iniquity." (Habak 1 v 13.)

We think of the angels as exalted beings, and far above ourselves; but we are told in Scripture, "He charged His angels with folly." (Job 4 v 18.) We admire the moon and stars as glorious and splendid bodies; but we read, "Behold even to the moon, and it shineth not, yea, the stars are not pure in His sight." (Job 25 v 5.)

We talk of the heavens as the noblest and purest part of creation; but even of them it is written, "The heavens are not clean in His sight." (Job 15 v 15.) What then is any one of us but a miserable sinner in the sight of such a God as this?

Surely we ought all to cease from proud thoughts about ourselves. We ought to lay our hands upon our mouths, and say with Abraham, "I am dust and ashes; "and with Job, "I am vile;" and with Isaiah, "We are all as an unclean thing;" and with John, "If we say that we have no sin we deceive ourselves and the truth is not in us." (Gen. 18 v 27; Job 40 v 4; Isaiah 64 v 6; 1 John 1 v 8.)

Where is the man or woman in the whole catalogue of the Book of Life, that will ever be able to say more than this, - "I obtained mercy"? What is the glorious company of the apostles, the goodly fellowship of the prophets, the noble army of martyrs, - what are they all but pardoned sinners? Surely there is but one conclusion to be arrived at: - We are all great sinners, and we all need a great forgiveness.

See now what just cause I have to say that to know our need of forgiveness is the first thing in true religion.

Sin is a burden, and must be taken off. Sin is a defilement, and must be cleansed away. Sin is a mighty debt, and must be paid. Sin is a mountain standing between us and heaven, and must be removed. Happy is that mother's child amongst us that feels all this!

The first step towards heaven is to see clearly that we deserve hell.

There are but two alternatives before us, - we must either be forgiven, or be miserable for ever.

See too how little most people know of the main design of Christianity, though they live in a Christian land. They fancy they are to go to church to learn their duty, and hear morality enforced, and for no other purpose. They forget that the heathen philosophers could have told them as much as this. They forget that such men as Plato and Seneca gave instructions which ought to put to shame the Christian liar, the Christian drunkard, and the Christian thief. They have yet to learn that the leading mark of Christianity is the remedy it provides for sin. This is the glory and excellence of the Gospel.

It meets man as he really is. It goes down to the level to which sin has brought him, and offers to raise him up. It tells him of a remedy equal to his disease, - a great remedy for a great disease, - a great forgiveness for great sinners.

I ask every reader to consider these things well, if you never considered them before. It is no light matter whether you know your soul's necessities or not:

it is a matter of life and death.

Try, I ask you, to become acquainted with your own heart. Sit down and think quietly what you are in the sight of God. Bring together the thoughts, and words, and actions of any day in your life, and measure them by the measure of God's Word. Judge yourself honestly, that you may not be condemned at the last day. Oh, that you might find out what you really are! Oh, that you might learn to pray Job's prayer: "Make me to know my transgression and my sin." (Job 13 v 23.) Oh, that you might see this great truth, - that until you are forgiven, your Christianity has done nothing for your at all!

2. Let me point out, in the second place, the way of forgiveness.

I ask particular attention to this point, for none can be more important. Granting for a moment that you want pardon and forgiveness, what ought you to do? Where will you go? Which way will you turn? Every thing hinges on the answer you give to this question.

Will you turn to ministers and put your trust in them?

They cannot give you pardon: they can only tell you where it is to be found. They can set before you the bread of life; but you yourself must eat it. They can show you the path of peace; but you yourself must walk in it.

The Jewish priest had no power to cleanse the leper, but only to declare him cleansed. The Christian minister has no power to forgive sins; - he can only declare and pronounce who they are that are forgiven.

Will you turn to sacraments and rites, and trust in them?

They cannot supply you with forgiveness, however diligently you may use them. By sacraments "faith is confirmed and grace increased," in all who rightly use them, but they cannot justify the sinner. They cannot put away transgression. You may go to the Lord's table every Sunday in your life: but unless you look far beyond the sign to the

thing signified, you will after all die in your sins.
You may attend a daily service regularly, but if you think to establish a righteousness of your own by it, in the slightest degree, you are only getting further away from God every day.

Will you trust in your own works and endeavours, your virtues and your good deeds, your prayers and your giving? They will never buy you an entrance into heaven. They will never pay your debt to God. They are all imperfect in themselves, and only increase your guilt. There is no merit or worthiness in them at the very best. The Lord Jesus Christ says expressly, "When you have done all those things which are commanded you, say, We are unprofitable servants." (Luke 17 v 10.)

Will you trust in your own repentance and reform? You are very sorry for the past. You hope to do better for time to come. You hope God will be merciful.

Alas, if you lean on this, you have nothing beneath you but a broken reed! The judge does not pardon the thief because he is sorry for what he did. Today's sorrow will not wipe off the record of yesterday's sins. It is not an ocean of tears that would ever cleanse an uneasy conscience and give it peace.

Where then must a man go for pardon? Where is forgiveness to be found? There is a way both sure and plain, and into that way I desire to guide every inquirer's feet.

That way is simply to trust in the Lord Jesus Christ as your Saviour. It is to cast your soul, with all its sins, unreservedly on Christ, - to cease completely from any dependence on your own works or doings, either in whole or in part, - and to rest on no other work but Christ's work, no other righteousness but Christ's righteousness, no other merit but Christ's merit, as your ground of hope.

Take this course and you are a pardoned soul. "To Christ", says Peter, "give all the prophets witness, that through His name whosoever believeth in Him shall receive remission of sins." (Acts 10 v 43.) "Through this Man," says Paul at Antioch, "is preached unto you the forgiveness of sins, and by Him all that believe are justified from all things" (Acts 13 v 38.) "In Him", writes Paul to the Colossians, "we have redemption through His blood , even the forgiveness of sins." (Col. 1 v 14.)

The Lord Jesus Christ, in great love and compassion, has made a full and complete satisfaction for sin, by suffering death in our place upon the cross. There He offered Himself as a sacrifice for us, and allowed the wrath of God, which we deserved, to fall on His own head. For our sins, as our

Substitute, He gave Himself, suffered, and died, - the just for the unjust, the innocent for the guilty, - that He might deliver us from the curse of a broken law, and provide a complete pardon for all who are willing to receive it.

And by so doing, as Isaiah says, He has borne our sins; as John the Baptist says,- He has taken away sin; as Paul says, - He has purged our sins, and put away sin; and as Daniel says, - He has made an end of sin, and finished transgression. (Isaiah 53 v 11; John 1 v 29; Heb. 1 v 3; Heb, 9 v 26; Dan. 9 v 24)

And now the Lord Jesus Christ is sealed and appointed by God the Father to be a Prince and a Saviour, to give remission of sins to all who will have it. The keys of death and hell are put in His hand. The government of the gate of heaven is laid on His shoulder. He Himself is the door, and by Him all that enter in shall be saved. (Acts 5 v 31; Rev. 1 v 18; John 10 v 9.)

Christ, in one word, has purchased a full forgiveness, if we are only willing to receive it.

He has done all, paid all, suffered all that was needful to reconcile us to God. He has provided a garment of righteousness to clothe us. He has opened a fountain of living waters to cleanse us. He has removed every barrier between us and God the Father, taken every obstacle out of the way, and made a road by which the vilest sinner may return. All things are now ready, and the sinner has only to believe and be saved, to eat and be satisfied, to ask and receive, to wash and be clean!

And faith, simple faith, is the only thing required, in order that you and I may be forgiven! That we will come by faith to

Jesus as sinners with our sins, - trust in Him, - rest on Him, - lean on Him, - confide in Him, - commit our souls to Him, - and forsaking all other hope, cleave only to Him, - this is all and everything that God asks for.
Let a person only do this, and they shall be saved. Their iniquities shall be found completely pardoned, and their transgressions entirely taken away.

Every man and woman that so trusts is wholly forgiven and reckoned perfectly righteous.

Their sins are clean gone, and their soul is justified in God's sight, however bad and guilty they may have been.

Faith is the only thing required, not knowledge.

A man may be a poor unlearned sinner, and know little of books. But if he sees enough to find the foot of the cross, and trust in Jesus for pardon, I tell you, from the authority of the Bible, that he shall not miss heaven.

To know Christ is the cornerstone of all religious knowledge.

Faith, I say, and not conversion. A man may have been walking in the broad way up to the very hour he first hears the Gospel. But if in that hearing he is awakened to feel his danger, and wants to be saved, let him come to Christ at once, and wait for nothing. That very coming is the beginning of conversion.

Faith, I repeat, and not holiness. A man may feel all full of sin, and unworthy to be saved. But let him not wait outside the ark till he is better. Let him come to Christ without delay, just as he is. Afterwards he shall be holy.

I call upon every reader of these pages to let nothing move him from this strong and steadfast ground, - that faith in Christ is the only thing needed for our justification.

Stand firm here, if you value your soul's peace. I see many walking in darkness and having no light, from confused notions as to what faith is. They hear that saving faith will work by love and produce holiness, and not finding all this at once in themselves, they think they have no faith at all.

They forget that these things are the fruits of faith, and not faith itself, and that to doubt whether we have faith, because we do not see them at once, is like doubting whether a tree is alive, because it does not bear fruit the very day we plant it in the ground. I charge you to settle it firmly in your mind, that in the matter of your forgiveness and justification there is but one thing required, and that is, simple faith in Christ.

I know well that the natural heart dislikes this doctrine. It runs counter to man's notions of religion. It leaves him no room to boast. Man's idea is to come to Christ with a price in his hand, - his church attendance, - his morality, - his repentance, - his good works, and so, as it were, to buy his pardon and justification. The Spirit's teaching is quite different: it is first of all, to believe. Whosoever believeth shall not perish. (John3 v 16.)

Some say such doctrine cannot be right, because it makes the way to heaven too easy. I fear that many such persons, if the truth were spoken, find it too hard.

I believe in reality it is easier to give a fortune in building a cathedral like York Minster, or to go to and be burned as a martyr, than thoroughly to receive "justification by faith" without the deeds of the law, and to enter heaven as a sinner saved by grace.

Some say this doctrine is foolishness and mere enthusiasm. I answer, This is just what was said of it some 2000 years ago, and it is a false charge now, as it was then. So far from the charge being true, a thousand facts can prove this doctrine to be from God.

No doctrine certainly has produced such mighty effects in the world, as the simple proclamation of free forgiveness through faith in Christ.

This is the glorious doctrine which was the strength of the Apostles when they went out to the Gentiles to preach a new religion. They began, a few poor fishermen, in a despised corner of the earth. They turned the world upside down. They changed the face of the Roman empire. They emptied the heathen temples of their worshippers, and made the whole system of idolatry crumble away. And what was the weapon by which they did it all? It was free forgiveness through faith in Jesus Christ.

This is the doctrine which brought light into Europe 500 years ago, at the time of the God-sent Reformation, and enabled one solitary monk, Martin Luther, to shake the whole Church of Rome. Through his preaching and writing the scales fell from men's eyes, and the chains of their souls were loosed. And what was the lever that gave him his power? It was free forgiveness through faith in Jesus Christ.

This is the doctrine which revived our own Church in the middle of last century, when Whitefield, and the Wesleys, and Berridge, and Venn broke up the wretched "spirit of slumber" which had come over the land (as also today), and roused men to think. They began a mighty work, with little seeming likelihood of success. They began, few in number, with small encouragement from the rich and great. But they prospered. And why? - Because they preached free forgiveness through faith in Christ.

This is the doctrine which is the true strength of any Church on earth at this day. It is not qualifications, or giftings, or fancy programmes, or learning, that will keep a church alive. Let free forgiveness through Christ be faithfully proclaimed in her pulpits and the gates of hell shall not prevail against her.
Let it be buried, or kept back, and her candlestick will soon be taken away. Let us never forget the brightest days of a Church are those when "Christ crucified" is most exalted.

The dens and caves of the earth, where the early Christians met to hear of the love of Jesus, were more full of glory and beauty in God's sight than ever was St. Peter's at Rome.
The meanest barn at this day, where the true way of pardon is offered to sinners, is a

far more honourable place than the Cathedral of Cologne or Milan. A Church is only useful so far as she exalts free forgiveness through Christ.

This is the doctrine which, of all others, is the mightiest engine for pulling down the kingdom on Satan.

The Greenlanders were unmoved so long as the Meravians told them of the creation and the fall of man; but when they heard of redeeming love, their frozen hearts melted like snow in spring.

Preach salvation by the sacraments, exalt the Church above Christ, and keep back the doctrine of the Atonement, and the devil cares little, - his goods are at peace. But preach a full Christ, and a free pardon by faith in Him, and then Satan will have great wrath, for he knows he has but a short time.

John Berridge said he went on preaching morality and nothing else till he found there was not a moral man in his parish. But when he changed his plan, and began to preach the love of Christ to sinners, and a free salvation by faith, then there was a stirring of the dry bones, and a mighty turning to God.

This is the only doctrine which will ever bring peace to an uneasy conscience, and rest to a troubled soul.

A man may get on pretty well without it so long as he is asleep about his spiritual condition. But once let him awake from his slumber, and nothing will ever calm him but the blood of Atonement, and the peace which comes by faith in Christ. How any one can undertake to be a minister of religion without a firm grasp of this doctrine, I never can understand. For myself, I can only say, I should think my office a most painful one if I had not the message of free forgiveness to convey. It would be miserable work indeed to visit the sick and dying, if I could not say, "Behold the Lamb of God: - believe on the Lord Jesus Christ, and thou shalt be saved."

The right hand of a Christian minister is the doctrine of free forgiveness through faith in Christ. Give us this doctrine, and we have power: we will never despair of doing good to men's souls.

Take away this doctrine, and we are weak as water. We may read the prayers and go through a round of ceremonies, but we are like Samson with his hair shorn: our strength is gone. Souls will not be benefited by us, and good will not be done.

I commend the things I have been saying to the notice of every reader. I am not ashamed of free pardon through faith in Christ, whatever some may say against the doctrine. I am not ashamed of it, for its fruits speak for themselves. It has done things that no other doctrine can ever do. It has effected moral changes which laws and punishments have failed to achieve, - which magistrates and policemen have laboured after in vain, - which psychiatric institutes and secular knowledge have proved utterly powerless to produce.

Just as the finest lunatics in Bethlehem hospital became suddenly gentle when kindly treated, even so the worst and most hardened sinners have often become as little children, when told of Jesus loving them and willing to forgive.

I can well understand Paul ending his Epistle to the erring Galatians with that solemn burst of feeling. "God forbid that I should glory, save in the cross of our Lord Jesus Christ." (Gal. 6 v 14.)

The crown has indeed fallen from a Christian's head when he leaves the doctrine of justification by faith.

You should ask yourself whether you have really received the truth which I have been dwelling on, and know it by experience. Jesus, and faith in Him, is the only way to the Father. He that thinks to climb into Paradise by some other road, will find himself fearfully mistaken.

Other foundation can no man lay for an immortal soul than that of which I have been freely speaking. He that ventures himself here is safe. He that is off this rock has got no standing ground at all.

You should seriously consider under what kind of a ministry you are in the habit of sitting. You have reason indeed to be careful. It is not all the same where you go, whatever people may say. There are many places of worship, I fear, where you might look long for Christ crucified, and never find Him. He is buried under outward ceremonies, - thrust behind the baptismal font, - lost sight of under the shadow of the Church. "They have taken away my Lord, and I know not where they have laid Him." (John 20 v 13.)

Take heed where you settle yourself. Try all by this single test, "Is Jesus and free forgiveness proclaimed here?"

There may be comfortable seats, - there may be good music, - there may be clever sermons. But if Christ's Gospel is not the sun and centre of the whole place, do not pitch your tent there. Say rather with Isaac, "Here is the wood and the fire, but where is the lamb?" (Gen. 22 v 7.) Be very sure this is not the place for your soul.

3. Let me, in the third place encourage all who wish to be forgiven.

I am quite sure that this paper will be read by some one who feels he is not yet a forgiven soul.

My heart's desire and prayer is that such an one may seek his pardon at once. And I would fain help him forward, by showing him the kind of forgiveness offered to him, and the glorious privileges within his reach.

Listen to me, then, while I try to exhibit to you the treasures of Gospel forgiveness. I cannot describe its fulness as I ought. Its riches are indeed unsearchable. (Eph. 3 v 8.) But if you turn away from it, you shall not be able to say in the day of judgment, you did not at all know what it was.

Consider, then, for one thing, that the forgiveness set before you is a great and broad forgiveness. Hear what the Prince of Peace Himself declares: "All sins shall be forgiven unto the sons of men, and blasphemies, wherewithsoever they shall blaspheme." (Mark 3 v 28.) "Though your sins be as scarlet, they shall become white as snow; though they be red like crimson, they shall be as wool." (Isaiah 1 v 18.)

Yes: though your trespass be more in number then the hairs on your head, the stairs in heaven, the leaves of the forest, the blades of grass, the grains of sand on the sea shore, still they can all be pardoned!

As the waters of Noah's flood covered over and hid the tops of the highest hills, so can the blood of Jesus cover over and hide your mightiest sins. "His blood cleanseth from all sin." (1 John 1 v 7.) Though to you they seem written with the point of a diamond, they can all be effaced from the book of God's remembrance by that precious blood.

Paul names a long list of abominations which the Corinthians had committed, and then says, "Such were some of you: but ye are washed." (1 Cor. 6 v 11.)

Furthermore, it is a *full and complete forgiveness.* It is not like David's pardon to Absalom, - a permission to return home, but not a full restoration to favour. (2 Sam. 14 v 24.) It is not, as some fancy, a mere letting off, and letting alone. It is a pardon so complete that he who has it is reckoned as righteous as if he had never sinned at all! His iniquities are blotted out.

They are removed from him as far as the east is from the west. (Psalm 103 v 12.) There remains no condemnation for him. The Father sees him joined to Christ, and is well pleased.

The Son beholds him clothed with His own righteousness, and says, "Thou are all fair, there is not spot in thee." (Song. 4 v 7.) Blessed be God that it is so! I truly believe if the best of us all had only one blot left for himself to wipe out, he would miss eternal life. If the holiest child of Adam were in heaven all but his little finger, and to get in depended on himself, I am sure he would never enter the kingdom.

If Noah, Daniel, and Job, had had but one day's sins to wash away, they would never have been saved. Praise be to God, that in the matter of our pardon there is nothing left for man to do!

Jesus does all, and man has only to hold out an empty hand and to receive.

Furthermore, it is a *free and unconditional forgiveness*. It is not burdened with an "if," like Solomon's pardon to Adonijah: "If he will show himself a worthy man." (1 Kings 1 v 52.) Nor yet are you obliged to carry a price in your hand, or to bring a character with you to prove yourself deserving of mercy. Jesus requires but one character, and that is that you should feel yourself a sinful, bad man. He invites you to "buy wine and milk without money and without price," and declares, "Whosoever will, let him take the water of life freely." (Isaiah 55 v 1; Rev. 22 v 17.)

Like David in the cave of Adullam, He receives every one that feels in distress and a debtor, and rejects none (1 Sam. 22 v 2.)

Are you a sinner? Do you want a Saviour? Then come to Jesus just as you are, and you soul shall live.

Again, it is an *offered forgiveness*. I have read of earthly Kings who knew not how to show mercy; of Henry the Eighth of England, who spared neither man nor woman, - of James the Fifth of Scotland, who would never show favour to a Douglas. The King of kings is not like them. He calls on men to come to Him, and be pardoned. "Unto you O men, I call, and my voice is to the sons of men." (Prov. 8 v 4.) "Ho! every one that thirsteth, come ye to the waters." (Isaiah 55 v 1.) "If any man thirst, let me come unto Me and drink." (John 7 v 37.) "Come unto Me, all yet hat labour and are heavy laden, and I will give you rest." (Matt. 11 v 28.) It ought to be a great comfort to you and me to hear of any pardon at all; but to hear Jesus Himself inviting us, to see Jesus Himself holding out His hand to us, - the Saviour seeking the sinner before the sinner seeks the Saviour, - this is encouragement, this is strong consolation indeed!

Again, it is *a willing forgiveness.* I have heard of pardons granted in reply to long entreaty, and wrung out by much importunity. King Edward the Third of England would not spare the citizens of Calais till they came to him with halters round their necks, and his own Queen interceded for them on her knees.

But Jesus is "good and ready to forgive." (Psalm 86 v 5.) He "delighteth in mercy."

(Micah 7 v 18.) Judgment is "His strange work." He is not willing that any should perish. (Isaiah 28 v 21, 2 Pet. 3 v 9.) He would have all men saved, and come to the knowledge of the truth. (1 Tim. 2 v 4.) He wept over unbelieving Jerusalem. "As I live," He says, "I have no pleasure in the death of the wicked. Turn ye, turn ye from your evil ways: why will ye die?" (Ezek. 33 v 11.) You and I may well come boldly to the throne of grace.

He who sits there is far more willing and ready to give mercy than we are to receive it. (Heb. 4 v 16.)

Besides this, it is *a tried and tested forgiveness.* Thousands and tens of thousands have sought for pardon at the mercy-seat of Christ, and not one has ever returned to say that he sought in vain. Sinners of every name and nation, - sinners of every sort and description, - have knocked at the door of the fold, and none have ever been refused admission. Zacchaeus the extortioner, Magdalen the harlot, Saul the persecutor, Peter the denier of his Lord, the Jews who crucified the Prince of Life, the idolatrous Athenians, the adulterous Corinthians, the ignorant Africans, the blood-thirsty New Zealanders, - all have ventured their souls on Christ's promises of pardon, and none have ever found them fail.

If the way which the Gospel sets before us were a new and untravelled way, we might well feel faint-hearted. But it is not so. It is an old path. It is a path worn by the feet of many pilgrims, and a path in which the footsteps are all one way.

The treasury of Christ's mercies has never been found empty. The well of living waters has never proved dry.

Besides this, it is *a present forgiveness*. All that believe in Jesus are at once justified from all things. (Acts 13 v 39.) The very day the younger son returned to his father's house he was clothed with the best robe, had the ring put on his hand, and the shoes on his feet. (Luke 15)

The very day Zacchaeus received Jesus he heard those comfortable words, "This day is salvation come to this house." (Luke 19 v 9.)

The very day that David said, "I have sinned against the Lord," he was told by Nathan, "The Lord also hath put away they sin." (2 Sam. 12 v 13.)

The very day you first flee to Christ, your sins are all removed. Your pardon is not a thing far away, to be obtained only after many months or years of sighing or contrition. It is near at hand. It is close to you, within your reach, all ready to be bestowed. Believe, and that very moment it is your own. "He that believeth is not condemned." (John 3 v 18.) It does not say,

"He shall not be," or "will not be," but "is not."

From the time of his believing, condemnation is gone. "He that believeth hath everlasting life." (John 3 v 36.) It does not say, "He shall have," or "will have," it is "hath" - "has eternal life!"

It is his own as surely as if he was in heaven, though not so evidently so to his own eyes. You must not think forgiveness will be nearer to a believer in the day of judgment than it was in the hour he first believed. His complete salvation from the power of sin is every year nearer and nearer to him; but as to his forgiveness and justification, and deliverance from the guilt of sin, it is a finished work from the very minute he first commits himself to Christ.

Last, and best of all, it is *an everlasting forgiveness*. It is not like Shimei's pardon, - a pardon that may some time be revoked and taken away. (1 Kings 2 v 9.) Once justified, you are justified for ever. Once written down in the book of life, your name shall never be blotted out. The sins of God's children are said to be cast into the depths of the sea, - to be sought for and not found, - to be remembered no more, - to be cast behind God's back. (Mic.7 v 19; Jer. 1 v 20; 31 v 34; Isa. 38 v 17.)

Some people fancy they may be justified one year and condemned another, - children of adoption at one time, and strangers again after a while, - heirs of the kingdom the beginning of their salvation, and yet servants of the devil in the end. I cannot find this in the Bible: - as the New Zealander told the Roman Catholic priest, "I do not see it in the Book."

It seems to me to overturn the good news of the Gospel altogether, and to tear up its comforts by the roots. I believe the salvation Jesus offers is an everlasting salvation, and pardon once sealed with His blood shall never be reversed.

I have set before you the nature of the forgiveness offered to you. I have told you but a little of it, for my words are weaker than my will. The half of it remains untold. The greatness of it is far more than any writings of mine. But I think I have said enough to show you it is worth the seeking, and I can wish you nothing better than that you may strive to make it your own.

Do you call it nothing to look forward to death without fear, and to judgment without doubtings, and to eternity without a sinking heart? Do you call it nothing to feel the world slipping from your grasp, and to see the grave getting ready for you, and the valley of the shadow of death opening before your eyes, and yet to be not afraid?

Do you call it nothing to be able to think of the great day of account, the throne, the books, the Judge, the assembled worlds, the revealing of secrets the final sentence, and yet to feel, "I am safe"? This is the portion, and this the privilege of a forgiven soul.

Such an one is *on a rock*. When the rain of God's wrath descends, and the floods come, and the winds blow, his feet shall not slide, his habitation shall be sure.

Such an one is *in an ark*. When the last fiery deluge is sweeping over all things on the surface of the earth, it shall not come near him. He shall be caught up, and borne securely above it all.

Such an one is in *a hiding place*. When God arises to judge terribly the earth, and men are calling to rocks and mountains to fall upon them and cover them, the Everlasting Arms shall be thrown around him, and the storm shall pass over his head. He shall "abide under the shadow of the Almighty." (Psalm 91 v 1.)

Such an one is *in a city of refuge.* The accuser of the brethren can lay no charge against him. The law cannot condemn him. There is a wall between him and the avenger of blood. The enemies of his soul cannot hurt him. He is in a secure sanctuary.

Such an one *is rich.* He has treasure in heaven which cannot be affected by worldly changes, compared to which New York and Hong Kong are nothing at all. He need not envy the richest merchants and bankers. He has an investment that will endure when bank-notes and gold are worthless things. He can say, like the Spanish ambassador, when shown the treasury at Venice, "My Master's treasury has no bottom."
He has Christ.

Such an one *is insured.* He is ready for anything that may happen. Nothing can harm him. Banks may break, and

Governments may be overturned. Famine and disease may rage around him. Sickness and sorrow may visit his own fireside. But still he is ready for all, - ready for health and happiness, - ready for tears, - ready for joy, - ready for hard times, - ready for plenty, - ready for life, - ready for death. He has Christ. He is a pardoned soul. "Blessed" indeed "is he whose transgression is forgiven, and whose sin is covered." (Ps. 32 v1.)

How will any one escape if he neglects so great salvation? Why should you not lay hold on it at once, and say, Pardon, me, even me also, O my Saviour! What would you have, if the way I have set before you does not satisfy you? Come while the door is open. Ask, and you shall receive.

4. Let me, in the last place, supply the readers of this paper with some marks of having found forgiveness.

I dare not leave out this point. Too many people presume they are forgiven, who have no evidence to show. Not a few cannot think it possible they are forgiven, who are plainly in the way to heaven, though they may not see it themselves. I would fain raise hope in some, and self-inquiry in others; and to do this, let me set down in order the leading evidences of a forgiven soul.

(a) Forgiven souls *hate sin*. They can enter most fully into the words of our Communion Service; "The remembrance of sin is grievous unto them, and the burden of it is intolerable."

It is the serpent which bit them: how should they not shrink from it with horror? It is the poison which brought them to the brink of eternal death how should they not loathe it with a godly disgust? It is the Egyptian enemy which kept them in hard bondage how should not the very memory of it be bitter to their hearts? It is the disease of which they carry the marks and scars about them, and from which they have scarcely recovered: well may they dread it, flee from it, and long to be delivered altogether from its power!

Remember how the woman in Simon's house wept over the feet of Jesus, (Luke 7 v 38) Remember how the Ephesians publicly burned their evil books. (Acts 19 v 19.) Remember how Paul mourned over his youthful transgressions: "I am not meet to be called an Apostle, because I persecuted the Church of God." (1 Cor. 15 v 9.)

If you and sin are friends, you and God are not yet reconciled. You are not fit for heaven; for one main part of heaven's excellence is the absence of all sin.

(b) Forgiven souls *love Christ*. This is that one thing they can say, if they dare say nothing else, - they do love Christ.

His person, His offices, His work, His name, His cross, His blood, His words, His example, His day, His ordinances, - all, all are precious to forgiven souls. The ministry which exalts Him most, is that which they enjoy most. The books which are most full of Him, are most pleasant to their minds. The people on earth they feel most drawn to, are those in whom they see something of Christ. His name is an ointment poured forth, and comes with a peculiar sweetness to their ears. (Song. 1 v 3.)

They would tell you they cannot help feeling as they do. He is their Redeemer, their Shepherd, their Physician, their King, their strong Deliverer, their gracious Guide, their hope, their joy, their All. Were it not for Him they would be of all men most miserable. They would as soon consent that you should take the sun out of the sky, as Christ out of their religion.

Those people who talk of "the Lord," and "the Almighty," and "the Deity," and so forth, but have not a word to say about Christ, are in anything but a right state of mind. What saith the Scripture? "He that honoureth not the Son, honoureth not the Father which hath sent Him." (John 5 v 23.) "If any man love not the Lord Jesus Christ, let him be anathema." (1 Cor. 16 v 22)

(c) Forgiven souls *are humble.* They cannot forget that they owe all they have and hope for to free grace, and this keeps them lowly. They are brands plucked from the fire, - debtors who could not pay for themselves, - captives who must have remained in prison for ever, but for undeserved mercy, - wandering sheep who were ready to perish when the Shepherd found them; and what right then have they to be proud?

I do not deny that there are proud saints. But this I do say, - they are of all God's creatures the most inconsistent, and of all

God's children the most likely to stumble and pierce themselves with many sorrows. Forgiveness more often produces the spirit of Jacob: "I am not worthy of the least of all the mercies, and all the truth which Thou has showed unto Thy servant" (Gen. 32 v 10); and of Hezekiah: - "I shall go softly all my years" (Isiah 38 v 15); and of the Apostle Paul: "I am less then the least of all saints, - chief of sinners." (Eph. 3 v 8; 1 Tim 1 v 15.) When you and I have nothing we can call our own but sin and weakness, there is surely no garment that becomes us so well as humility.

(d) Forgiven souls *are holy*. Their chief desire is to please Him who has saved them, to do His will, to glorify Him in body and in Spirit, which are His. "What shall I render unto the Lord for all His benefits?" (Ps. 116 v 12), is a leading principle in a pardoned heart. It was the remembrance of Jesus showing mercy that made Paul so abundant in his work, and in doing good so untiringly.

It was a sense of pardon that made Zaccheus say, "The half of my goods I give to the poor, and if I have taken anything from any man by false accusation, I restore him four-fold." (Luke 19 v 8.)

If any one points out to me believers who are in a carnal slothful state of soul, I reply in the words of Peter, "They have forgotten they were purged from their old sins." (2 Pet. 1 v 9.) But if you show me a man deliberately living an unholy and licentious life, and yet boasting that his sins are forgiven, I answer, "He is under a ruinous delusion, and is not forgiven at all." I would not believe he is forgiven if an angel from heaven affirmed it, and I charge you not to believe it too.

Pardon of sin and love of sin are like oil and water, - they will never go together. All that are washed in the blood of Christ are also sanctified by the Spirit of Christ.

(e) Forgiven souls *are forgiving*. They do as they have been done by. They look over the offences of their brethren. They endeavour to "walk in love, as Christ loved them, and gave Himself for them." (Eph. 5 v 2.)

They remember how God for Christ's sake forgave them, and endeavour to do the same towards their fellow-creatures. Has He forgiven them pounds, and shall they not forgive a few pence? Doubtless in this, as in every thing else, they come short;- but this is their desire and their aim.

A spiteful quarrelsome Christian is a scandal to his profession. It is very hard to believe that such an one has ever sat at the foot of the cross, and has ever considered how he is praying against himself every time he uses the Lord's Prayer. Is he not saying as it were, "Father, do not forgive me my trespasses at all"? But it is still harder to understand what such a one would do in heaven, if he got there. All ideas of heaven in which forgiveness has not a place, are castles in the air and vain fancies.

Forgiveness is the way by which every saved soul enters heaven. Forgiveness is the only title by which he remains in heaven.
Forgiveness is the eternal subject and song of all the redeemed who inhabit heaven. Surely an unforgiving soul in heaven would find his heart completely out of tune. Surely we know nothing of Christ's love to us but the name of it, if we do not love our brethren.

I lay these things before every reader of this paper. I know well there are great diversities in the degree of men's attainments in grace, and that saving faith in Christ is consistent with many imperfections. But still I do believe the five marks I have just been naming will generally be found more or less in all forgiven souls.

I cannot conceal from you, these identifications should raise in many minds great searchings of heart. I must be plain. I fear there are thousands of persons called Christians, who know nothing of these identifications. They are baptized. They attend the services of their Church. They would not on any account be reckoned infidels. But as to true repentance and saving faith, union with Christ and sanctification of the Spirit, they are "names and words" of which they know nothing at all.

Now if this paper is read by such persons, it will probably either alarm them, or make them very angry. If it makes them angry I shall be sorry. It alarms them I shall be glad. I want to alarm them. I want to awaken them from their present state. I want them to take in the great fact, they are not yet forgiven, that they have not peace with God, and are on the high road to destruction.

I must say this, for I see no alternative. It seems neither Christian faithfulness, nor Christian love, to keep it back. I see certain hall-marks of pardoned souls laid down in Scripture. I see an utter want of these marks in many men and women around me. How then can I avoid the conclusion that they are not yet "forgiven"?

And how shall I do the work of a faithful watchman if I do not write it down plainly in so many words? What is the use of crying Peace! Peace! when there is no peace? Where is the honesty of acting the part of a lying physician, and telling people there is no danger, when in reality they are fast drawing near to eternal death?

Surely the blood of souls would be required at my hands if I wrote to you anything less than the truth. "If the trumpet give an uncertain sound, who shall prepare himself to the battle?" (1 Cor. 14 v 8.)

Examine yourself, then, before this subject is forgotten. Consider of what sort your religion is. Try it by the five marks I have just set before you. I have endeavoured to make them as broad and general as I can, for fear of causing any heart to be sad that God has not made sad.
If you know anything of them, though it be but a little, I am thankful, and entreat you to go forward. But if you know nothing of them in your own experience, let me say, in all affection, I stand in doubt of you. I tremble for your soul.

1. And now, before I conclude, let me put a home question to every one who reads this

paper. It shall be short and plain, but it is all important: "Are you forgiven?"

I have told you all I can about forgiveness. Your need of forgiveness, - the way of forgiveness, - the encouragements to seek forgiveness, - the marks of having found it, - all have been placed before you.

Bring the whole subject to bear upon your own heart, and ask yourself, "Am I forgiven? Either I am, or I am not. Which of the two is it?"

You believe perhaps, there is forgiveness of sins. You believe that Christ died for sinners, and that He offers a pardon to the most ungodly. But are you forgiven yourself? Have you yourself laid hold on Christ by faith, and found peace through His blood?
What profit is there to you in forgiveness, except you get the benefit of it?

What does it profit the shipwrecked sailor that the life-boat is alongside, if he sticks by the wreck, and does not jump in and escape?
What does it avail the sick man that the doctor offers him a medicine, if he only looks at it, and does not swallow it down?

Except you lay hold for your own soul, you will be as surely lost as it there was no forgiveness at all.

If ever your sins are to be forgiven, it must be *now*, - now in this life, if ever in the life to come, - *now* in this world, if they are to be found blotted out when Jesus comes again the second time. There must be actual business between you and Christ. Your sins must be laid on Him by faith: His righteousness must be laid on you. His blood must be applied to your conscience, or else your sins will meet you in the day of judgment, and sink you into hell.

Oh, how can you trifle when such things are at stake? How can you be content to leave it uncertain whether you are forgiven?

Surely that a man can make his will, insure his life, give directions about his funeral, and yet leave his soul's affairs in uncertainty, is a reckless thing indeed.

2. Let me next give a solemn warning to every one who reads this paper, and knows in his conscience he is not forgiven.

Your soul is in awful danger. You may die this year. And if you die as you are, you are lost for ever. If you die without pardon, without pardon you will rise again at the last day. There is a sword over your head which hangs by a single hair. There is but a step between you and death. Oh, I wonder that you can sleep quietly in your bed!

You are not yet forgiven. Then what have you got by your religion? You go to church.

You have a Bible, you have a Prayer-book, and perhaps a Hymn-book. You hear sermons. You join in services. It may be you go to the Lord's table. But what have you really got after all? Any hope? Any peace? Any joy? Any comfort? Nothing: literally nothing! You have got nothing but mere temporal things, if you are not a pardoned soul.

You are not yet forgiven. But you trust God will be merciful. Yet why should He be merciful if you will not seek Him in His own appointed way? Merciful He doubtless is, wonderfully merciful to all who come to Him in the name of Jesus. But if you choose to despise His directions, and make a road to heaven of your own, you will find to your cost there is no mercy for you.

You are not yet forgiven. But you hope you will be some day. I cannot put up with that expression. It is like thrusting off the hand of conscience, and seizing it by the throat to stop its voice. Why are you more likely to seek forgiveness at a future time? Why should you not seek it now? Now is the time for gathering the bread of life. The day of the Lord is fast drawing near, and then no man can work. (Exod. 16 v 26.) The Seventh trumpet will soon sound. The kingdoms of this world will soon become the kingdoms of our Lord and of His Christ. (Rev. 11 v 15.) Woe to the house which is found without the scarlet line, and without the mark of blood upon the door! (Joshua 2 v 18; Exod. 17 v 13.)

Well, you may not feel your need of forgiveness now, but a time may come when you will want it.

The Lord in mercy grant that it may not then be too late, for the Bible says that God will not always strive with you. God gives time and opportunity for you to respond, but there comes a time when, through the hardness of your own heart, you cease to hear His call. Today is the day of salvation. There may never be another one for you.

3. Let me next give an earnest invitation to all who read this paper and desire forgiveness.

I know not who you are, or what you have been in time past, but I say boldly, Come to Christ by faith, and you shall have a pardon. High or low, rich or poor, young men and young women, old men and children, -you cannot be worse than Manasseh and Paul before conversion, - than David and Peter after conversion: come all of you to Christ, and you shall be freely forgiven.

Do not think for a moment that you have some great thing to do before you come to Christ. Such a notion is of the earth, earthy; the Gospel bids you come just as you are.

Man's idea is to make his peace with God by repentance, and then come to Christ at last: the Gospel way is to receive peace from Christ first of all, and begin with Him.

Man's idea is to amend, and turn over a new leaf, and so work his way up to reconciliation and friendship with God: the Gospel way is first to be friends with God through Christ, and then to work.

Man's idea is to toil up the hill, and find life at the top: the Gospel way is first to live by faith in Christ, and then to do His will.

And you decide, you decide, which is true Christianity? Which is the good news? Which is the glad tidings? First the fruits of the Spirit and then peace, or first peace and then the fruits of the Spirit? First sanctification and then pardon, or first pardon and then sanctification? First service and then life, or first life and then service? Your own hearts can well supply the answer.

Come then, willing to receive, and not thinking how much you can bring. Come, willing to take what Christ offers, and not fancying you can give anything in return.

Come with your sins, and no other qualifications but a hearty desire for pardon, and, as sure as the Bible is true, you shall be saved.

You may tell me you are not worthy, you are not good enough, you are not chosen. I answer, You are a sinner, and you want to be saved, and what more do you want?

You are one of those whom Jesus came to save. Come to Him and you shall have life.

Take with you words, and He will hear you graciously. Tell Him all your soul's necessities, and I know from the Bible He will answer you. Tell Him you have heard that He receives sinners, and that you are such. Tell Him you heard He has the keys of life in his hand, and entreat Him to let you in.

Tell Him you come in dependence on His promises, and ask Him to fulfill His word, and "do as He has promised." (2 Sam. 7 v 25.)

Do this in simplicity and sincerity, and I promise you, you shall not ask in vain. Do this and you shall find Him faithful and just to forgive your sins, and to cleanse you from all unrighteousness (1 John 1 v 9.)

4. Last of all, let me give a word of exhortation to all forgiven souls.

You are forgiven. Then know the full extent of your privileges, and learn to rejoice in the Lord. You and I are great sinners, but then we have a great Saviour.

You and I have sinned sins that are past man's knowledge, but then we have "the love of Christ, which passeth knowledge," to rest upon. (Eph. 3 v 19.) You and I feel our hearts to be a bubbling fountain of evil, but then we have another fountain of greater power in Christ's blood, to which we may daily resort. You and I have mighty enemies to contend with, but then the "Captain of our salvation" is mightier still, and is with us forever.

Why should our hearts be troubled? Why should we be disquieted and cast down? O men and women of little faith that we are!

Why do we doubt?

Let us strive every year to grow in grace, and in the knowledge of our Lord Jesus Christ. It is sad to be content with a little religion. It is honourable to desire the best gifts. We ought not to be satisfied with the same kind of hearing, and reading, and praying, which satisfied us in years gone by.

We ought to labour every year to throw more heart and reality into everything we do in our Christian walk. To love Christ more intensely, - to hate evil more thoroughly, - to cleave to what is good more closely, - to watch even our least ways more narrowly, - to declare very plainly that we seek a country, - to put on the Lord Jesus Christ, and be clothed with Him in every place and company, to see more, - to feel more, - to know more, - to do more, - these ought to be our aims and desires every year we begin. Truly there is room for improvement in us all.

Let us try to do good to the souls of others, more than we have done up to now. Alas, it is poor work indeed to be swallowed up in our own spiritual concerns, and taken up with our own spiritual ailments, and never to think of others! We forget that there is such a thing as religious selfishness.

Let us count it a sorrowful thing to go to heaven alone, and let us seek to draw companions with us. We ought never to forget that every man, woman and child around us, will soon be either in heaven, or hell.

Let us say to others, as Moses did to Hobab, "Come with us, and we will do thee good." (Num. 10 v 29.) Oh, it is indeed a true saying, "He that watereth shall be watered himself". (Prov. 11 v 25.) The idle, do-little, selfish Christian has little idea what he is missing.

But above all, let us learn to live in the life of faith in Jesus more than we have so far. Ever to be found by the fountain side, - ever to be eating Christ's body by faith, and drinking Christ's blood by faith, - ever to have before our minds Christ's dying for our sins, - Christ's rising again for our justification, - Christ interceding for us at God's right hand, - Christ soon coming again to gather us to Himself, - this is the mark which we should have continually before our eyes. We may fall short, but let us aim high. Let us walk in the full light of the Sun of righteousness, and then our graces will grow.

Let us not be like trees on a cold north wall, weak, half-starved, and unfruitful. Let us rather strive to be like the sun-flower, and follow the great Fountaiin of Light wherever He goes, and see Him with open face.

Oh, for an eye more quick to discern His dealings! Oh, for an ear more ready to hear His voice!

Finally, let us say to everything in the world that interferes between ourselves and Jesus Christ, "Stand´ aside;" and let us dread permitting ourselves the least evil habits, in case they rise up like a mist and hide Him from our eyes.

"In His light alone shall we see light" and feel warmth, and away from Him we shall find the world a dark and cold wilderness. (Psalm 36 v 9.) We should call to mind the request of the Athenian philosopher, when the mightiest Monarch on earth asked him what he desired most. "I have," said he, "but one request to make; and that is that you would stand from between me and the sun." [or, if you like, " Get out of my light"] Let us think lightly of the world's gifts. Let us sit calmly under its cares. Let us care for nothing if we may only ever see the King's face, if we may only ever abide in Christ.

If our sins are forgiven, the best things are yet to come. Yet a little time, and we shall "see face to face, and know as we have been known." We shall "see the King in His beauty," and "go out no more." (1 Cor. 13 v 12; Isa. 33 v 17; Rev. 3 v 12.) "Blessed then is he whose transgression is forgiven, and whose sins are covered" (Psalm 32 v 1.)

THE CROSS OF CHRIST.

THE CROSS OF CHRIST.

"God forbid that I should glory, save in the cross of our Lord Jesus Christ" GAL. 6 v 14.

What do we think and feel about the cross of Christ?

We live in a so-called 'Christian' country.

We probably attend the worship of a Christian church. We have, most of us, been baptised in the name of Christ. We profess and call ourselves Christians. All this is well: it is more than can be said of millions in the world. But *what do we think and feel about the* cross of Christ?

I want to examine what one of the greatest Christians that ever lived thought of the cross of Christ. He has written down his opinion: he has given his judgment in words that cannot be mistaken. The man I mean is the Apostle Paul.

The place where you will find his opinion, is in the letter which the Holy Ghost inspired him to write to the Galatians. The words in which his judgment is set down, are these, "God forbid that I should glory, save in the cross of our Lord Jesus Christ."

Now what did Paul mean by saying this? He meant to declare strongly, that he trusted in nothing but "Jesus Christ crucified" for the pardon of his sins and the salvation of his soul. Let others, if they would, look elsewhere for salvation; let others, if they were so disposed, trust in other things for pardon and peace: for his part the apostle was determined to rest on nothing, lean on nothing, build his hope on nothing, place confidence in nothing, glory in nothing, except " the cross of Jesus Christ."

I wish to say something about "the cross" to the readers of this volume. Believe me, the subject is one of the deepest importance.

This is no mere question of controversy. It is not one of those points on which men may agree to differ, and feel that differences will not shut them out of heaven

A man must be right on this subject, or he is lost for ever. Heaven or hell, happiness or misery, life or death, blessing or cursing in the last day, - all hinges on the answer to this question: "What do you think about the cross of Christ?"

1. Let me show you, first of all, what the Apostle Paul did not glory in.

There are many things that Paul might have gloried in, if he had thought as some do in this day. If ever there was one on earth who had something to boast of in himself, that man was the great apostle of the Gentiles. Now if he did not dare to glory, who shall?

He never gloried in his national privileges. He was a Jew by birth, and, as he tells us himself, - "An Hebrew of the Hebrews." (Phil. 3 v 5.) He might have said, like many of his brethren, "I have Abraham for my forefather I am not a dark unenlightened heathen; I am one of the favoured people of God: I have been admitted into covenant with God by circumcision. I am a far better man than the ignorant Gentiles."

But he never said so. He never gloried in anything of this kind. Never, for one moment!

He never gloried in his own works. None ever worked so hard for God as he did. He was "more abundant in labours" than any of the apostles. (2 Cor. 11 v 23.) No man ever preached so much, travelled so much, and endured so many hardships for Christ's cause.

None was ever made the means of converting so many souls, did so much good to the world, and made himself so useful to mankind.

No Father of the early Church, no Reformer, no Puritan, no Missionary, no minister, no layman, - no one man could ever be named, who did so many good works as the Apostle Paul. But did he ever glory in them, as if they were in the least meritorious, and could save his soul? Never! Never for one moment!

He never gloried in his knowledge.
He was a man of great gifts naturally, and, after he was converted, the Holy Spirit gave him greater gifts still. He was a. mighty preacher, and a mighty speaker, and a mighty writer. He was as great with his pen as he was with his tongue. He could reason equally well with Jews and Gentiles. He could argue with infidels at Corinth, or Pharisees at Jerusalem, or self-righteous people in Galatia. He knew many deep things. He had been in the third heaven, and "heard unspeakable words." (2 Cor. 12 v 4.

He had received the spirit of prophecy, and could foretell things yet to come. But did he ever glory in his knowledge, as if it could justify him before God ? Never: never! Never for one moment!

He never gloried in his graces.

If ever there was one who abounded in graces, that man was Paul. He was full of love. How tenderly and affectionately he used to write! He could feel for souls like a mother or a nurse feeling for her child. He was a bold man. He cared not whom he opposed when truth was at stake. He cared not what risks he ran when souls were to be won.

He was a self-denying man, - in hunger and thirst often, in cold and nakedness, in watchings and fastings.

He was a humble man. He thought himself less than the least of all saints, and the chief of sinners. He was a prayerful man. See how it comes out at the beginning of all his Epistles. He was a. thankful man. His thanksgivings and his prayers walked side by side. But he never gloried in all this, - never prided himself on it, - never rested his soul's hopes on it. Oh, no: not for a moment!

He never gloried in his Church attendance. If ever there was a good churchman, that man was Paul. He was himself a chosen apostle. He was a founder of churches, and an ordainer of ministers: Timothy and Titus, and many elders, received their first commission from his hands.

He was the beginner of services and meetings in many a dark place. Many did he baptize; many did he receive to the Lord's Table; many a meeting for prayer, and praise, and preaching, did he begin and carry on. He was the setter up of discipline in many a young Church. Whatever ordinances, and rules, and ceremonies were observed in many churches, were first recommended by him.

But did he ever glory in his office and church standing? Does he ever speak as if his Churchmanship would save him, justify him, put away his sins, and make him acceptable before God? oh, no! Never: never! Never for a moment!

Now if the apostle Paul never gloried in any of these things, who in all the world, from one end to the other, - who has any right to glory in them in our day? If Paul said, "God forbid that I should glory in anything whatever except the cross," who shall dare to say, "I have something to glory of: I am a better man than Paul"?

Who is there among the readers of this paper that trusts in any goodness of their own? Who is there that is resting on his own amendments, - his own morality, - his own churchmanship, his own works and performances of any kind whatever?

Who is there that is leaning the weight of his soul on anything whatever of his own, in the smallest possible degree? Learn, I say, that you are very unlike the apostle Paul. Learn that your religion is not *apostolical religion*

Who is there among the readers of this paper that trusts in his religious profession for salvation?

Who is there that is rating himself on his baptism, or his attendance at the Lord's table, - his church-going on Sundays, or his daily services during the week, - and saying to himself, "What do I yet lack?" Learn, I say, this day, that you are very unlike Paul. Your Christianity is not the Christianity of the New Testament. Paul would not glory in anything but "the cross." Neither ought you.

Oh, let us beware of self-righteousness!

Open sin kills its thousands of souls. Self-righteousness kills its tens of thousands. Go and study humility with the great apostle of the Gentiles. Go and sit with Paul at the foot of the cross. Give up your secret pride. Cast away your vain ideas of your own goodness. Be thankful if you have grace, but never glory in it for a moment. Work for God and Christ, with heart and soul and mind and strength, but never dream for a second of placing confidence in any work of your own.

Think, you who take comfort in some fancied ideas of your own goodness, -

think, you who wrap up yourselves in the notion, "all must be right, if I keep to my Church," - think for a moment what a sandy foundation you are building upon! Think how miserably defective your hopes and pleas will look in the hour of death, and in the day of judgment!

Whatever men may say of their own goodness while they are strong and healthy, they will find but little to say of it when they are sick and dying. Whatever merit they may see in their own works here in this world, they will discover none in them when they stand before the bar of Christ. The light of that great day of judgment will make a wonderful difference in the appearance of all their doings. - It will strip off the tinsel, shrivel up the complexion, expose the rottenness of many a deed that is now called good. Their wheat will prove nothing but chaff: their gold will be found nothing but dross.

Millions of so-called Christian actions vill turn out to have been utterly defective and graceless. They appeared good, and were valued among men: they will prove light and worthless in the balance of God. They will be found to have been like the whitened graves of old, - fair and beautiful on the outside, but full of corruption within.

Alas, for the man who can look forward to the day of judgment, and lean his soul in the smallest degree on anything of his own now!

Once more I say, let us beware of self-righteousness in every possible shape and form. Some people get as much harm from their fancied virtues as others do from their sins. Rest not till your heart beats in tune with St. Paul's. Rest not till you can say with him, "GOD FORBID THAT I SHOULD GLORY IN ANYTHING BUT THE CROSS."

2. Let me explain, in the second place, *what we are to understand by the cross of Christ.*

The cross is an expression that is used in more than one meaning in the Bible. What did St. Paul mean when he said, "I glory in the cross of Christ," in the Epistle to the Galatians? This is the point I now wish to examine closely and make clear.

The cross sometimes means that wooden cross, on which the Lord Jesus Christ was nailed and put to death on Calvary. This is what St. Paul had in his mind's eye, when he told the Philippians that Christ "became obedient unto death, even the death of the cross." (Phil. 2 v 8.)

This is not the cross in which St. Paul gloried. He would have shrunk with horror from the idea of glorying in a mere piece of wood. I have no doubt he would have denounced the Roman Catholic adoration of the crucifix, as profane, blasphemous, and idolatrous.

The cross sometimes means the afflictions and trials which believers in Christ have to go through, if they follow Christ faithfully, for their religion's sake. This is the sense in which our Lord uses the word when He says, "He that taketh not his cross and followeth after Me, cannot be my disciple." (Matt. 10 v 38.) This also is not the sense in which Paul uses the word when he writes to the Galatians. He knew that cross well: he carried it patiently. But he is not speaking of it here.

But the cross also means, in some places, the doctrine that Christ died for sinners upon the cross, - the atonement that He made for sinners, by His suffering for them on the cross, - the complete and perfect sacrifice for sin which He offered up, when He gave His own body to be crucified.

In short, this one word, "the cross," stands for Christ crucified, the only Saviour. This is the meaning in which Paul uses the expression, when he tells the Corinthians, "the preaching of the cross is to them that perish foolishness." (1 Cor. 1 v 18.) This is the meaning in which he wrote to the Galatians, "God forbid that I should glory, save in the cross." He simply meant, "I glory in nothing but Christ crucified, as the salvation of my soul."

Jesus Christ crucified was the joy and delight, the comfort and the peace, the hope and the confidence, the foundation and the resting-place, the ark and the refuge, the food and the medicine of Paul's soul. He did not think of what be had done himself, and suffered himself. He did not meditate on his own goodness, and his own righteousness.

He loved to think of what Christ had done, and Christ had suffered, - of the death of Christ, the righteousness of Christ, the atonement of Christ, the blood of Christ, the finished work of Christ. In this he did glory. This was the sun of his soul.

This is the subject he loved to preach about. He was a man who went to and fro on the earth, proclaiming to sinners that the Son of God had shed His own heart's blood to save their souls. He walked up and down the world telling people that Jesus Christ had loved them, and died for their sins upon the cross.

Mark how he says to the Corinthians, "I delivered unto you first of all that which I also received, how that Christ died for our sins." (1 Cor. 15 v 3.) "I determined not to know anything among you save Jesus Christ, and Him crucified." (1 Cor. 2 v 2.)

He, a blaspheming, persecuting Pharisee, had been washed in Christ's blood. He could not hold his peace about it. He was never weary of telling the story of the cross.

This is the subject he loved to dwell upon when he wrote to believers. It is wonderful to observe how full his epistles generally are of the sufferings and death of Christ - how they run over with "thoughts that breathe and words that burn," about Christ's dying love and power.

His heart seems full of the subject. He enlarges on it constantly: he returns to it continually. It is the golden thread that runs through all his doctrinal teaching and practical exhortations. He seems to think that the most advanced Christian can never hear too much about the cross of Christ.

This is what he lived upon all his life, from the time of his conversion.

He tells the Galatians, "The life that I now live in the flesh I live by the faith of the Son of God who loved me and gave Himself for me." (Galatians 2 v 20)

What made him so strong to labour? What made him so willing to work? What made him so tireless in endeavouring to save some? What made him so persevering and patient? I will tell you the secret of it all. He was always feeding by faith on Christ's body and Christ's blood. Jesus crucified was the meat and drink of his soul. And we may rest assured that Paul was right.

Depend upon it, the cross of Christ, - the death of Christ on the cross to make atonement for sinners, - is the centre truth in the whole Bible. This is the truth we begin with when we open Genesis. The seed of the woman bruising the serpent's head is nothing else but a prophecy of Christ crucified. - This is the truth that shines out, though veiled, all through the law of Moses, and the history of the Jews. The daily sacrifice, the Passover lamb, the continual shedding of blood in the tabernacle and temple, - all these were emblems of Christ crucified.

This is the truth that we see honoured in the vision of heaven before we close the book of' Revelation. "In the midst of the throne and of the four beasts," we are told, "and in the midst of the elders, stood a Lamb as it had been slain." (Rev. 5 v 6.)

Even in the midst of heavenly glory we get a view of Christ crucified.. Take away the cross of Christ, and the Bible is a dark book. It is like the Egyptian hieroglyphics without the key that interprets their meaning, - curious and wonderful, but of no real use.

Let every reader of this paper mark what I say. You may know a good deal about the Bible. You may know the outlines of the histories it contains, and the dates of the events described, just as a man knows the history of England. You may know the names of the men and women mentioned in it, just as a man knows Caesar, Alexander the Great, or Napoleon. You may know the several precepts of the Bible, and admire them, just as a man admires Plato, Aristotle, or Seneca. But if you have not yet found out that Christ crucified is the foundation of the whole volume, you have read your Bible up to now with very little profit.

Your religion is a heaven without a sun, a compass without a needle, a clock without spring or weights, a lamp without oil. It will not comfort you. It will not deliver your soul from hell.

Mark what I say again. You may know a good deal about Christ, by a kind of head knowledge. You may know who He was, and where He was born, and what He did.

You may know His miracles, His sayings, His prophecies, and His words. You may know how He lived, and how He suffered, and how He died. But unless you know the power of Christ's cross by experience, - unless you know and feel within that the blood shed on that cross has washed away your own particular sins, - unless you are willing to confess that your salvation depends entirely on the work that Christ did upon the cross, - unless this be the case, Christ will profit you nothing.

The mere knowing Christ's name will never save you. You must know His cross, and His blood, or else you will die in your sins.

As long as you live, beware of a religion in which there is not much of the cross. You live in times when the warning is sadly needful. Beware, I say again, of a religion without the cross.

There are hundreds of places of worship, in this day, in which there is everything almost except the cross. There is carved oak, and sculptured stone; there is stained glass, and brilliant painting; there are a host concerts, plays, performances, and a constant round of conferences; There are artists, choirs, actors, and there are 'entertainments'; but the real cross of Christ is not there.

Jesus crucified is not proclaimed in the pulpit.

The Lamb of God is not lifted up, and salvation by faith in Him is not freely proclaimed. And all is wrong.

Beware of such places of worship. They are not apostolical. They would not have satisfied St. Paul.

There are thousands of religious books published in our times, in which there is everything except the cross. They are full of stories, and praises of men. They abound in exhortations about holy livings and rules for the attainment of perfection. They have plenty of Christian symbols, both inside and outside.

But the real cross of Christ is left out. The Saviour, and His work of atonement and complete salvation, are either not mentioned, or mentioned in an unscriptural way. And hence they are worse than useless. Beware of such books. They are not apostolical They would never have satisfied St. Paul.

St. Paul gloried in nothing but the cross. Strive to be like him. Set Jesus crucified fully before the eyes of your soul. Do not listen to any teaching which would place anything between you and Him. Do not fall into the old Galatian error: do not think that any one in this day is a better guide than the apostles.

Do not be ashamed of the "old paths," in which men walked who were inspired by the Holy Ghost. Let not the vague talk of modern teachers, who speak great swelling words about "unity," and "the ministry," disturb your peace, and make you loose your hands from the cross.

Churches, ministers, and sacraments, are all useful in their way, but they are not Christ crucified. Do not give Christ's honour to another "He that glorieth, let him glory in the Lord." (1 Cor. 1 v 1.)

3. Let me show, lastly, *why all Christians ought to glory in the cross of Christ.*

I feel that I must say something on this point, because of the ignorance that prevails about it. I suspect that many see no peculiar glory and beauty in the subject of Christ's cross. On the contrary, they think it painful, humbling, and depressing. They do not see much profit in the story of His death and sufferings They rather turn from it as an unpleasant thing. They would rather talk of *prosperity*, or *kingdom-building*, or *church-growth*.

Now I believe that such persons are quite wrong. I cannot hold with them. I believe it is an excellent thing for us all to be continually dwelling on the cross of Christ. It is a good thing to be often reminded how Jesus was betrayed into the hands of wicked men, - how they condemned Him with the most unjust judgment, - how they spat on Him, scourged Him, beat Him, and crowned Him with thorns, - how they led Him forth as a lamb to the slaughter, without His murmuring or resisting, - how they drove the nails through His hands and feet, and set Him up on Calvary between two thieves, - how they pierced His side with a spear, mocked Him in His sufferings, and let Him hang there naked and bleeding till He died.

Of all these things, I say, it is good to be reminded. It is not for nothing that the crucifixion is described four times over in the New Testament. There are very few things that all four writers of the Gospel describe.

Generally speaking, if Matthew, Mark, and Luke tell a thing in our Lord's history, John does not tell it. But there is one thing that all the four give us most fully, and that one thing is the story of the cross. This is a telling fact, and not to be overlooked.

People seem to me to forget that all Christ's sufferings on the cross were fore-ordained. They did not come on Him by chance or accident: they were all planned, counselled, and determined from all eternity. The cross was foreseen in all the provisions of the everlasting Trinity for the salvation of sinners. In the purposes of God the cross was set up from everlasting. Not one throb of pain did Jesus feel, not one precious drop of blood did Jesus shed, which had not been appointed long ago. Infinite wisdom planned that redemption should be by the cross. Infinite wisdom brought Jesus to the cross in due time. He was crucified "by the determinate counsel and foreknowledge of God." (Acts 2 v 23.)

People seem to me to forget that all Christ's sufferings on the cross were necessary for man's salvation. He had to bear our sins, if ever they were to be borne at all. With His stripes alone could we be healed. This was the one payment of our debt that God would accept: this was the great sacrifice on which our eternal life depended. If Christ had not gone to the cross and suffered in our stead, the just for the unjust, there would not have been a spark of hope for us. There would have been a mighty gulf between ourselves and God, which no man ever could have passed.

People seem to me to forget that all Christ's sufferings were endured voluntarily, and of His own free will. He was under no compulsion. Of His own choice He laid down His life: of His own choice He went to the cross in order to finish the work He came to do.

He might easily have summoned legions of angels with a word, and scattered Pilate and Herod, and all their armies, like chaff before the wind. But He was a willing sufferer. His heart was set on the salvation of sinners. He was resolved to open "a fountain for all sin and uncleanness," by shedding His own blood. (Zech. 13 v 1.)

When I think of all this, I see nothing painful or disagreeable in the subject of Christ's cross. On the contrary, I see in it wisdom and power, peace and hope, joy and gladness, comfort and consolation. The more I keep the cross in my mind's eye, the more fulness I seem to discern in it. The longer I dwell on the cross in my thoughts, the more I am satisfied that there is more to be learned at the foot of the cross than anywhere else in the world.

(a) Would I know the length and breadth of God the Father's love towards a sinful world?

Where shall I see it most displayed?

Shall I look at His glorious sun shining down daily on the unthankful and evil? Shall I look at seed-time and harvest, returning in regular yearly succession? Oh, no! I can find a stronger proof of love than anything of this sort.

I look at the cross of Christ.

I see in it not the cause of the Father's love, but the effect. Where I see that God so loved this wicked world, that He gave His only begotten Son, - gave Him to suffer and die, - that "whosoever believeth in Him should not perish, but have eternal life." (John 3 v 16.) I know that the Father loves us, because He did not withhold from us His Son, His only Son.

I might sometimes fancy that God the Father is too high and holy to care for such miserable, corrupt creatures as we are! But I cannot, must not, dare not think it, when I look at the cross of Christ.

(b) Would I know how exceedingly sinful and abominable sin is in the sight of God?

Where shall I see that most fully brought out?

Shall I turn to the history of the flood, and read how sin drowned the world? Shall I go to the shore of the Dead Sea, and mark what sin brought on Sodom and

Gomorrah? Shall I turn to the wandering Jews, and observe how sin has scattered them over the face of the earth? No: I can find a clearer proof still!

I look at the cross of Christ. There I see that sin is so black and damnable, that nothing but the blood of God's own Son can wash it away. There I see that sin has so separated me from my holy Maker, that all the angels in heaven could never have made peace between us. Nothing could reconcile us, short of the death of Christ. If I listened to the wretched talk of proud men, I might sometimes fancy sin was not so very sinful!

But I cannot think little of sin, when I look at the cross of Christ

(c) Would I know the *fullness and completeness* of the salvation God has provided for sinners?
Where shall I see it most distinctly?

Shall I go to the general declarations in the Bible about God's mercy? Shall I rest in the general truth that God is a "God of love"? Oh, no! I will look at the cross of Christ. I find no evidence like that. I find no balm for a sore conscience and a troubled heart, like the sight of Jesus dying for me on the accursed tree. There I see that a full payment has been made for all my enormous debts.

The curse of that law which I have broken has come down on One who there suffered in my stead. The demands of that law are all satisfied. Payment has been made for me, even to the uttermost farthing. It will not be required twice over.

Ah, I might sometimes imagine I was too bad to be forgiven! My own heart sometimes whispers that I am too wicked to be saved. But I know in my better moments this is all my foolish unbelief. I read an answer to my doubts in the blood shed on Calvary. I feel sure that there is a way to heaven for the very vilest of men, when I look at the cross.

(d) Would I find strong reasons *for being a holy man*?

Where shall I turn for them?

Shall I listen to the ten commandments merely? Shall I study the examples given me in the Bible of what grace can do? Shall I meditate on the rewards of heaven, and the punishments of hell? Is there no stronger motive still?

Yes: I will look at the cross of Christ! There I see the love of Christ constraining me to "live not unto myself, but unto Him." There I see that I am not my own now: I am "bought with a price." (2 Cor. 5 v 15; 1 Cor. 6 v 20.)
I am bound by the most solemn obligations to glorify Jesus with body and spirit, which are His.

There I see that Jesus gave Himself for me, not only to redeem me from all iniquity, but also to purify me, and to make me one of a "peculiar people, zealous of good works." (Titus 2 v 14.) He bore my sins in His own body on the tree, "that I being dead unto sin should live unto righteousness." (1 Pet. 2 v 24.)
There is nothing so sanctifying as a clear view of the cross of Christ! It crucifies the world unto us, and us unto the world. How

can we love sin, when we remember that because of our sins Jesus died? Surely none ought to be so holy as the disciples of a crucified Lord.

(e) Would I learn how *to be contented and cheerful* under all the cares and anxieties of life? What school shall I go to?

How shall I attain this state of mind most easily? Shall I look at the sovereignty of God, the wisdom of God, the providence of God, the love of God? It is well to do so. But I have a better argument still. I will look at the cross of Christ. I feel that "He who spared not His only-begotten Son, but delivered Him up to die for me, will surely with Him give me all things" that I really need. (Rom. 8 v 32.)

He that endured such agony, sufferings, and pain for my soul, will surely not withhold from me anything that is really good. He that has done the greater things for me, will doubtless do the lesser things also. He that gave His own blood to procure me a home in heaven, will unquestionably supply me with all that is really profitable for me by the way. There is no school for learning contentment that can be compared with the foot of the cross!

(f) Would I gather *arguments for hoping that I shall never be cast away?* Where shall I go to find them?

Shall I look at my own graces and gifts? Shall I take comfort in my own faith, and love, and penitence, and zeal, and prayer? Shall I turn to my own heart, and say "this same heart will never be false and cold"?

Oh, no! God forbid! I will look at the cross of Christ. This is my grand argument. This is my main stay. I cannot think that He who went through such sufferings to redeem my soul, will let that soul perish after all, when it has once cast itself on Him.

Oh, no! what Jesus paid for, Jesus will surely keep. He paid dearly for it. He will not let it easily be lost. He called me to Himself when I was a dark sinner: He will never forsake me after I leave believed. When Satan tempts us to doubt whether

Christ's people will be kept from falling, we should tell Satan to look at the cross.

And now, will you marvel that I said all Christians ought to glory in the cross? Will you not rather wonder that any can hear of the cross and remain unmoved?

I declare I know no greater proof of man's depravity, than the fact that thousands of so-called Christians see nothing in the cross. Well may our hearts be called stony, - well may the eyes of our mind be called blind, - well may our whole nature be called diseased, - well may we all be called dead, when the cross of Christ is heard of and yet neglected.

Surely we may take up the words of the prophet, and say, "Hear, O heavens, and be astonished O earth; a wonderful and a horrible thing is done," - Christ was crucified for

"The believer is so freed from eternal wrath, that if Satan and conscience say, "Thou art a sinner, and under the curse of the law," he can say, It is true, I am a sinner; but I was hanged on a tree and died, and was made a curse in my Head and Lawgiver Christ, and His payment and suffering is my payment and suffering" *Rutherford's Christ Dying. 1647.*

sinners, and yet many Christians live as if He was never crucified at all!

(a) *The cross is the grand peculiarity of the Christian religion.* Other religions have laws and moral precepts, forms and ceremonies, rewards and punishments.

But other religions cannot tell us of a dying Saviour.

They cannot show us the cross. This is the crown and glory of the Gospel. This is that special comfort which belongs to it alone.

Miserable indeed is that religious teaching which calls itself Christian, and yet contains nothing of the cross.

A man who teaches in this way, might as well profess to explain the solar system, and yet tell his hearers nothing about the sun.

(b) *The cross is the strength of a minister.*
I for one would not be without it for all the world. I should feel like a soldier without arms, - like an artist without his pencil, - like

a pilot without his compass, - like a labourer without his tools.

Let others, if they will, preach the law and morality; let others hold forth the terrors of hell, and the joys of heaven; let others drench their congregations with teachings about the sacraments and the church; give me the cross of Christ! This is the only lever which has ever turned the world upside down up to now, and made men forsake their sins. And if this will not, nothing will.

A man may begin preaching with a perfect knowledge of Latin, Greek, and Hebrew; but he will do little or no good among his hearers unless he knows something of the cross.

Never was there a minister who did much for the conversion of souls who did not dwell much on Christ crucified. Luther, Rutherford, Whitefield, M'Cheyne, were all most eminently preachers of the cross. This is the preaching that the Holy Ghost delights to bless. He loves to honour those who honour the cross.

(c) *The cross is the secret of all missionary and evangelistic success.*

Nothing but this has ever moved the hearts of the unsaved.

Just according as this has been lifted up missions have prospered. This is the weapon which has won victories over hearts of every kind, in every quarter of the globe. Greenlanders, Africans, South-Sea Islanders, Hindus, Chinese, all have alike felt its power.

Just as that iron tube which crosses the Menai Straits, is more affected and bent by half-an-hour's sunshine than by all the dead weight that can be placed in it, so in like manner the hearts of savages have melted before the cross, when every other argument seemed to move them no more than stones.

"Brethren," said a North-American Indian after his conversion, "I have been a heathen. I know how heathens think. Once a preacher came and began to explain to us that there was a God; but we told him to return to the place from whence he came. Another preacher came and told us not to lie, nor steal, nor drink; but we did not heed him.

At last another came into my hut one day and said, "I am come to you in the name of the Lord of heaven and earth. He sends me to let you know that He will make you happy, and deliver you from misery. For this end He became a man, gave His life a ransom, and shed His blood for sinners."

I could not forget his words. I told them to the other Indians, and an awakening began among us. I say, therefore, preach the sufferings and death of Christ, our Saviour, if you wish your words to gain entrance among the heathen."

Never indeed did the devil triumph so thoroughly, as when he persuaded the Jesuit missionaries in China to keep back the story of the cross!

(d) *The cross is the foundation of a Church's prosperity.*

No church will ever be honoured where Christ crucified is not continually lifted up:

nothing whatever can make up for the want of the cross.

Without it all things may be done decently and in order; without it there may be splendid ceremonies, beautiful music, gorgeous churches, learned ministers, crowded communion tables, huge collections for the poor. But without the cross no good will be done; dark hearts will not be enlightened, proud hearts will not be humbled, mourning hearts will not be comforted, fainting hearts will not be cheered.

Sermons about unity, anointing, and apostolic ministry, - sermons about baptism and the Lord's supper, - sermons about fasting, tything, and communion, - sermons about great men and saints, - such sermons will never make up for the absence of sermons about the cross of Christ. They may amuse some: they will feed none. A gorgeous banqueting room, and splendid gold plate on the table, will never make up to a hungry man for the want of food.

Christ crucified is God's ordinance for doing good to men. Whenever a Church keeps back Christ crucified, or puts anything whatever in that foremost place which Christ crucified should always have, from that moment a Church ceases to be useful.

Without Christ crucified in her pulpits, a church is little better than an obstacle in the path, a dead carcass, a well without water, a barren fig tree, a sleeping watchman, a silent trumpet, a dumb witness, an ambassador without terms of peace, a messenger without tidings, a lighthouse without a light, a stumbling-block to weak believers, a comfort to villains, a hot-bed for formalism, a joy to the devil, and an offence to God.

(e) *The cross is the grand centre of union among true Christians.*

Our outward differences are many, without doubt. One Man is a Charismatic, another is a Pentecostal, - one is an Independent, another a Baptist, - one is a Calvinist, another an Armenian, - one is a Lutheran, another a Plymouth Brother, - but, after all, what shall we hear about most of these differences, in heaven? Nothing, most probably: nothing at all.

Does a man really and sincerely glory in the cross of Christ? That is the grand question. If he does, he is my brother: we are travelling on the same road; we are journeying towards a home where Christ is all, and everything outward in religion will be forgotten. But if he does not glory in the cross of Christ, I cannot feel comfort about him. Union on outward points only is union only for a time: union about the cross is union for eternity. Error on outward points is only a skin-deep disease: error about the cross is disease at the heart. Union about outward points is a mere man-made union: union about the cross of Christ can only be produced by the Holy Ghost.

I know not what you think of all this. I feel as if I had said nothing compared to what might be said. I feel as if the half of what I desire to tell you about the cross were left untold. But I do hope that I have given you something to think about. I do trust that I have shown you that I have reason for the question with which I began this paper: "What do you think and feel about the cross of Christ?"

Listen to me now for a few moments, while I say something to apply the whole subject to your conscience.

(a) *Are you living in any kind of sin?*

Are you following the course of this world, and neglecting your soul? Listen to what I say to you this day: "Behold the Cross of Christ." See there how Jesus loved you!

See there what Jesus suffered to prepare for you a way of salvation. Yes, careless men and women, for you that blood was shed! For you those hands and feet were pierced with nails! For you that body hung in agony on the cross! You are those whom Jesus loved, and for whom He died!

Surely that love ought to melt you. Surely the thought of the cross should draw you to repentance. Oh, that it might be so this very day! Oh, that you would come at once to that Saviour who died for you, and is willing to save! Come, and cry to Him with the prayer of faith, and I know that He will listen. Come, and lay hold upon the cross, and I know that He will not cast you out.

Come, and believe on Him who died on the cross, and this very day you shall have eternal life. How will you ever escape if you neglect so great salvation ? None surely will be so deep in hell as those who despise the cross!

(b) *Are you inquiring the way towards heaven?*

Are you seeking salvation, but doubtful whether you can find it? Are you desiring to have an interest in Christ, but doubting whether Christ will receive you? To you also I say this day, "Behold the cross of Christ." Here is encouragement if you really want it. Draw near to the Lord Jesus with boldness, for nothing need keep you back. His arms are open to receive you: His heart is full of love towards you. He has made a way by which you may approach

Him with confidence. Think of the cross. Draw near, and fear not.

(c) *Are you an unlearned man*?

Are you desirous to get to heaven, and perplexed and brought to a stand-still by difficulties in the Bible which you cannot explain? To you also I say this day, "Behold the cross of Christ." Read there the Father's love and the Son's compassion. Surely they are written in great plain letters, which none can well mistake.

What if you are now perplexed by the doctrine of election? What though at present you cannot reconcile your own utter corruption and your own responsibility? Look, I say, at the cross.

Does not that cross tell you that Jesus is a mighty, loving, ready Saviour? Does it not make one thing plain, and that is that it is all your own fault if you are not saved? Oh, get hold of that truth, and hold it fast!

(d) *Are you a believer that longs to be more holy?*

Are you one that finds his heart too ready to love earthly things? To you also I say, "Behold the cross of Christ." Look at the cross, think of the cross, meditate on the cross, and then go and set your affections on the world if you can. I believe that holiness is nowhere learned so well as on Calvary. I believe you cannot look much at the cross without feeling your will sanctified, and your tastes made more spiritual.

As the sun gazed upon makes everything else look dark and dim, so does the cross darken the false splendour of this world.

As honey tasted makes all other things seem to have no taste at all, so does the cross seen by faith take all the sweetness out of the pleasures of the world. Keep on every day steadily looking at the cross of Christ, and you will soon say of the world, as the poet does, -

Its pleasures now no longer please,
No more content afford;
Far from my heart be joys like these,
Now I have seen the Lord.

As by the light of opening day
The stars are all concealed,
So earthy pleasures fade away
When Jesus is revealed.

(e) *Are you a dying believer?*

Have you gone to that bed from which something within tells you you will never come down alive? Are you drawing near to that solemn hour, when soul and body must part for a season, and you must launch into a world unknown? Oh, look steadily at the cross of Christ by faith, and you shall be kept in peace!
Fix the eyes of your mind firmly, not on a man-made crucifix, but on Jesus crucified, and He shall deliver you from all your fears. Should you walk through dark places, He will be with you. He will never leave you, - never forsake you. Sit under the shadow of the cross to the very last, and its fruit shall be sweet to your taste.

"Ah," said a dying missionary, "there is but one thing needful on a death-bed, and that is to feel one's arms around the cross!"

I lay these thoughts before your mind. What you think now about the cross of Christ, I cannot tell. But I can wish you nothing better than this, - that you may be able to say with the Apostle Paul, before you die or meet the Lord, "God forbid that I should glory, save in the cross of our Lord Jesus Christ."